MW01127224

Living**Faith**

Prayers *for* Catholics

Living Faith: *Prayers for Catholics* was compiled by Julia DiSalvo and Kasey Nugent for Creative Communications for the Parish, 1564 Fencorp Drive, Fenton, MO 63026. 800-325-9414.

www.livingfaith.com
www.creativecommunications.com

ISBN: 978-1-889387-93-2

Cover and interior photographs: Shutterstock.com
Cover and interior design: Jamie Wyatt

Printed in the U.S.A.

Table of Contents

Foreword

Prayer, according to the classical definition, is "the raising of the heart and mind to God." Since God is closer to us than we are to ourselves, praying should be fairly easy, and sometimes it is—but not always.

When prayer becomes difficult, we appreciate simple remedies like the classic prayers of our youth and the Rosary. We may like to see how someone else prays—one of the saints perhaps, or a writer who seems like a kindred spirit. However we choose to pray, it is worth remembering that the desire has been planted in us by a God who always listens and responds.

The prayers presented here will allow you to respond to God's invitation in a variety of ways. Look them over and find the ones that resonate with you. May they lead you to form your own prayers or even to silent contemplation. Wherever the Holy Spirit leads you, you will be blessed.

Mark Neilsen, retired editor of Living Faith

Acknowledgments

The Morning, Evening, Seasonal and other situational prayers in this book, plus the "St. Joseph Prayer" and Stations of the Cross meditations, were written for *Living Faith: Daily Catholic Devotions* and Creative Communications for the Parish. We especially thank Denise Barker, Mitch Finley, Steve Givens, Jean Royer, Nancy F. Summers and Sr. Marguerite Zralek, OP, for their contributions.

Most of the traditional Catholic prayers in this book have slight variations and reside in the public domain. Their sources are varied—saints, Scripture, tradition. When known, the authors are listed.

Scripture passages are from the *New Revised Standard Version Bible: Catholic Edition*, © 1989, 1993 National Council of the Churches of Christ in the United States of America. Used by permission. All rights reserved.

Morning
Prayers

O Lord Jesus Christ, for the sake of your Name, the early missionaries set out to spread the Good News. O Jesus, my friend, teacher and companion, I set out today to find you in my busy world. That isn't always easy—sometimes it's hard just to find you in my own heart! Help me begin this day with faith that you are with me and with those I meet today. AMEN.

Lord, this is a day I have been waiting for, and I pray that it will be a day that gives you glory. I know I have certain expectations of this day, but I also want to pray that your will be done in all things. Help me to be aware of my own desires and preferences, but always willing to accept whatever is your will for my life. Grant me the joy and the freedom of the saints who understood that in following you, we will find every good thing. AMEN.

Lord Jesus, thank you for the gift of another day. When I am tempted to take the blessings of my life for granted, remind me that you have provided all that I need—not just for today but for my eternal salvation. There are no accidents in your loving plans, but we don't always understand how everything works for our benefit. May I be grateful to you for everything this day, for the little things and for the gift of life itself. AMEN.

Loving God, I give thanks to you for this new day. Give me the grace to follow through on my commitments and obligations—be they large or small—but especially those I have made to you. Thank you for being at my side and in my heart.

AMEN.

Lord of heaven and earth, by your power and for your glory the sun has come up another day. Thank you for the gift of life renewed throughout the universe. I offer this day to you. May all that I do, say and think be for your greater glory. AMEN.

Good and gracious God, I know you have blessed me beyond measure throughout all my days. Give me confidence in your care as I strive to fulfill the obligations I face today, those I can now anticipate and those that will come unexpectedly. May I recognize your presence in the people I meet and the opportunities I face. AMEN.

The dawn of a new day brings with it fresh possibilities, through your mercy, O Lord. Fill me not with regret over yesterday or worry about tomorrow, but confidence and courage to live in the freedom of the present moment. Here you abide with me in a foretaste of eternal life. Open my heart to receive the good gifts you will offer me today, sure to be enough to sustain me. I ask this through Jesus Christ, your Son and our Lord.

AMEN.

Almighty God and Father, I pray this morning especially for the particular needs of my loved ones. May you pour out your merciful love on them to give them strength in the obligations and trials they face. May they draw closer to you in faith hope and love. AMEN.

Lord Jesus, you came to give us life to the full, and each day you fulfill your promise. Help me to accept your will for me today in the people I encounter, the events I experience and in the quiet of my heart at rest in you. May I be filled with gratitude when the day comes to its end. AMEN.

Lord, this morning I am filled with hope for what the day will bring. Be with me as I go about my activities and keep me mindful of your love and care. Thank you for the opportunities you have given me, and may I always act according to your will. AMEN.

Gracious God, thank you for including me in your marvelous work of creation. As the sun rises this morning, may I turn my attention to you so that I might receive the gift of a new day in gratitude. May I pause throughout the day, especially at mealtimes, to give you thanks for the nourishment and the time to enjoy it. May I seek your presence in all things, especially in other people, be they family, friends, strangers or even enemies. Through Jesus Christ I ask all these things. AMEN.

Lord, as the sun rises in the morning sky, I take this moment to renew the vows of my baptism. I reject Satan and all the attractions of evil. I desire to follow your will in all things. Help me to grow in trust in your providential care and to remember that I may never know the good I do for others when I serve you. AMEN.

Lord, help me to remember that each day is a new opportunity to serve you and so to get closer to the source of true joy. I know there will be many prudent decisions of all kinds I have to make, but help me to think of how best to serve you. AMEN.

O Lord, show me the path for my life so that I might be able to do your will throughout this day. Be my guide when I am confused, my strength when I waver and my courage when I am afraid.

AMEN.

Jesus, be near me in this bustle of activity and noise today. When I become absorbed in myself, turn my attention to you and to the needs of those around me so that I can give away some of the goodness you have given me. Show me the right path for the remainder of this day and refresh me so I can go on renewed to try to do your will. Help me to remember that you are the Source of all life, the Judge of all success and the Measure of all that is good. AMEN.

Praise to you, O Lord, for the dawn of a new day. May the same Spirit that gives life to all of

creation give me new life today. Open my heart
in welcome to all that you wish to give me today.
Bless the people I will encounter and help me to
be an ambassador of your love for them. I pray that
I may do your holy will in all things, through Jesus
Christ, my Lord. AMEN.

Lord, in the song of the birds I hear your delight
in all of creation. In the warmth of the sunlight
and the rain, I feel your care for all living things.
In this new day, help me to let go of what happened yesterday and avoid too much concern
about what will happen tomorrow. You have given
me life this day, and with it I have everything I
need to be happy. Help me to see my blessings and
appreciate them. AMEN.

Lord, I have obligations that I need to fulfill
today, but to tell you the truth, I am not looking
forward to it. I do, however, want to trust that all
things will work together for good through your
loving providence. May the mysterious action
of the Holy Spirit transform all my actions into
greater glory for you and for the salvation of the
whole world. AMEN.

Lord, give me a heart filled with gratitude as this morning unfolds. When I am inclined to see "the same old thing," remind me that each moment comes from your hand, fresh with possibility and new hope. May I never take for granted the people you put in my life, but graciously receive the blessing of their presence and humbly learn from them, according to your will. AMEN.

Jesus, even in the freshness of morning, it is all too easy to take another day for granted. Help me to savor this moment and to cherish the gift of life, even in difficult times. I know that your promises are the only guarantees life holds for us. So help me to appreciate what I have, especially the people you have put in my life. May I never lose sight of how precious my time with them really is. AMEN.

Jesus, truly God, truly human, you know the challenges we all face as we strive to do your will. As this new day unfolds help me to respond to the promptings of your Holy Spirit so that I can be a channel of your love. Give me the strength and courage I need to complete the work that is set out before me. May I find joy in being united with you in all things. AMEN.

Lord Jesus, I awake this morning aware of people who need my prayers, and so I bring them to you in hope and trust that you will give them what they need. I especially ask that you give them a sense of your presence and love. At the same time, strengthen me to be your presence to everyone I meet today. Slow me down so that I can recognize opportunities to serve others in your name. AMEN.

Lord, you have given us this day as an opportunity to draw close to you. As I prepare for the activities ahead, I take this moment to accept your gift and ask that you give me the grace I need to be transformed into the person you want me to be. I know this may not happen all at once, but in this moment I surrender to your will. When I stray, lead me back to you. AMEN.

You, O Lord, created me in your image and in every moment you bless all that I am. All creation reflects your love for me and teaches me to trust in your protection. When I feel vulnerable, help me to follow your will. When I move out of my comfort zone, help me pour myself out for others as Jesus did. AMEN.

Precious Lord, I have awakened to this day with a new awareness of your love for me. Bless my preparations for what I have to do today. Grant me, I pray, the grace to hear the whispering of the Holy Spirit guiding me in thought, word and action. Wherever my path leads me, I trust in you. AMEN.

Spirit of the Living God, blow gently on the embers of my faith and ignite the light of faith in my heart for all to see. When I am tempted to hide this light and find an easier path to walk, remain at my side, close to me, nudging me forward. As the morning unfolds, renew my strength with your grace. For the day is long and without you I am weak. AMEN.

Lord Jesus, thank you for the gift of another day. In your wisdom and providence, you have set before me the responsibilities and challenges that I will face today. Help me to accept the fact that I am not perfect and so cannot respond perfectly. Help me to receive the courage and strength to do what needs to be done with generosity and compassion. Send your Holy Spirit to me in my darkest moments so that I know I am never alone. AMEN.

In the quiet of these first morning moments, Lord, I give you thanks for all that I have been given. May these gifts remind me that I need fear no evil and that I can freely share what I have, knowing that you will not abandon me in my need. Help me to be generous, especially with my time. Amen

Lord, in this quiet moment of prayer I can see the day spread out before me, and I know it may be a long while before I think of you again. My days are a whirlwind of activity, and today promises to be another one of those days. But I will try to keep you in my heart whenever I can, and I ask only that you be with me, even if I am too rushed to be aware of it. I praise and thank you for all your good gifts to me. AMEN.

Lord Jesus, I pray that you will refresh me today as you have once again refreshed the whole world with a new dawn. Renew my zeal for my faith and give me a sense of wonder for the simple experiences of the day: washing my hands, drinking a cup of coffee, hearing the voice of someone I know. Help me to praise you in all things and to serve you by serving others. AMEN.

Thank you, Lord, for the gift of another day.
I know that your grace sustained me at every
moment, whether I was aware of it or not. As I
look back over all that I experienced today, may
the Holy Spirit show me where I acted according
to your will and where I failed to do so. In your
mercy, heal my faults and strengthen me in virtue
for all my tomorrows. AMEN.

Lord, thank you for your gift of life and for the
many blessings I have enjoyed today. Thank you
for sustaining me in hope as I faced the day's challenges. Please give me a good night's sleep, but if
I am wakeful, Lord, help me to keep watch with
you and offer my restlessness for all those who are
grieving tonight. AMEN.

Lord, this was a hard, frustrating day, and it left
me feeling unsettled and unfulfilled. I seemed to
run up too many blind alleys and experience too
much impatience. Help me to trust in your goodness despite these setbacks. Though I cannot see
the fruits of my labor today, give me the confidence
to remember that your providential wisdom extends
much further than my own limited sight. AMEN.

Lord Jesus, you invited us to come to you when we are burdened and to receive rest. Take the day's weariness from me so that I can relax and be ready for sleep. Thank you for the support you gave me today as I tried to take your yoke upon my shoulders. For the times I resisted and turned away from your help, I ask forgiveness. May the gift of sleep restore me and make me ready to walk with you once again tomorrow. AMEN.

Gracious God, my mind is filled tonight with memories of what has happened and concerns about what is to come. Much of what fills my heart right now I can do nothing about, and tomorrow is soon enough to take action where it is needed. Now is the time for rest, and so I place myself in your hands and trust in your mercy. Grant me a good night's sleep, secure in your eternal love for me. AMEN.

Thank you, Lord Jesus, for all the gifts of this day, especially those I have not noticed. Help me to see where I have fallen short of true discipleship so that I can ask forgiveness and receive your healing mercy. As this day draws to a close, give my spirit deep rest and confidence in you so that I can rise tomorrow renewed in faith, hope and love. AMEN.

Father in heaven, you have given us the night as a time for rest, and you know how much I need it today. You also know that sometimes slumber can be hard to come by, and the minutes go by slowly when I cannot sleep. I ask you for a good night's sleep, but even more, I ask that you fill me, awake or asleep, with a sense of your loving presence. AMEN.

Almighty and Eternal God, your forgiveness and love give me peace at the end of this day. With every breath I take, your love fills me with hope. The night enfolds me in darkness, while your Spirit illuminates my memory of all that I have experienced today. Help me to discern in these experiences what I need to learn in order to best serve your will. AMEN.

Blessed Lord, I reflect tonight on all the lives your love has touched and transformed. What I have witnessed cannot come close to all you have made possible this day. Bless those who go to bed hungry tonight, wrap the children without beds in your loving arms and welcome those who pass away tonight to new life. AMEN.

Dearest Father, you continue to bless all life on earth with everything we need. This abundance from your heart calls us to a more generous stewardship. Bless those who call on you for help, and change our hearts that we may do a better job of caring for people in need. Grant me the grace to live with enough and want for nothing more than your love. AMEN.

Blessed Giver of Life, you know the length of our days, and you call on us to trust you in all things. Open my heart to your presence as this day draws to a close. In your mercy, help me to reflect upon today to see how I might have served you better and how I responded well to the call to follow Jesus. Take my sins away and grant me a good night's rest. AMEN.

Dear Lord, this was a discouraging day, for reasons I don't fully understand. Much of it was beyond my control, but I am not clear about how I might have made things any better. Tonight I just want to place my discouragement in your hands, for you have far more compassion and understanding than I. In the words of St. Ignatius, give me only your love and your grace, and that will be enough for me. Amen.

Thank you, God, for all this day has brought me. As I now spend a few moments looking back on all that has happened today, send your Holy Spirit to show me how you were at work in my life. For those times, I am grateful. For the times I turned away from you and ignored your will, I am sorry. In the hope of your mercy, I commend myself to you and take my rest. Amen.

Lord, free me from the cares of the day so that I can receive much needed rest. Let me not worry about all that is out of my control but instead trust in you. I pray that tomorrow will present new opportunities to change what I can and to accept what I cannot. I place my hope in you and pray that I will never be parted from you. AMEN.

Dear Jesus, bless me with a good night's sleep. Take away the cares of the day, for there is nothing I can do about them now anyway—except pray. And so, Lord, I ask you to look into my heart and see what lies heavy there. In your mercy and wisdom, take away these burdens and set things right, if that be your will. May I rise in the morning refreshed and ready to work for your greater glory and praise. AMEN.

After a long day, I am bone-tired and filled with weariness. Heavenly Father, I am in need of rest, so I pray in confidence that you will give me what I need most. Set my mind and heart at rest so that my body can relax and enjoy a deep sleep. Be with me the whole night through so that I will be renewed and restored to face another day with hope and courage. AMEN.

Dear God, this has been a long day. You know
well the struggles of my heart, my inner doubts
and disappointments. You know how often I have
turned to you and asked for the grace to change
for the better. And you know how often I have
turned away from your help and gone my own way.
Tonight I ask forgiveness for my failures. I ask once
again for the grace to search for happiness only
through you. Give me the peace of knowing that
you will ever be with me, no matter how many
times I fail. AMEN.

Jesus, my Lord and Brother, be with me tonight.
Take my worries and fears upon yourself, and let
me rest with a tranquil heart. I hope that I have
done all that I could do today. I pray now from the
bottom of my heart for those I love and for those
I need to learn to love. I pray also for myself that
I may turn my cares over to you, for your love and
care is deeper than I can imagine. AMEN.

Dear Lord, I pray that in the darkness and silence of this night, I will always be aware of how close you are to me. Help me to have a good night's sleep, but if I am wakeful, remind me to call upon you and say, "Speak, Lord, your servant is listening." If you wish to tell me anything, may I listen carefully. If you respond with silence, may I trust that your silence is filled with love and affection. Thank you, Lord, for all your goodness to me. May I never doubt your love. AMEN.

As the daylight fades into twilight, O Lord, I rest in the promise of your mercy. As the sun sets, be with me and fill my heart with love. Though darkness settles all around me, the light of your Spirit dispels my fear. I thank you for all you have given me this day. Bless my slumber with peace. AMEN.

Lord, I call to mind your presence and I pray in great gratitude for this day. Though it did not all turn out as I had expected or hoped, still I know that you are with me, and that is enough. I can see where I might have made better choices, and for that I ask your forgiveness. I can also see where you touched me through other people and through the goodness of the world. For that I thank you. Now I ask that you help me to put the day aside and find rest this night, secure in your love for me and for all those I love. AMEN.

Lord, as I look back upon the day, show me your hand in the blessings I enjoyed. Reveal yourself in the simple joys of a cool drink or a gentle breeze. Remind me that you were present even in moments of distress when I felt uncomfortable, frightened or angry. Teach me how I might have acted better so that when the opportunity comes again, I might love others more as you do. I give you thanks for every good thing and ask your blessing on my rest tonight. AMEN.

Seasonal
Prayers

Advent (1)

Loving Creator of the Universe, we ask your help as we begin this season of joyful expectation. Give us the longing of your prophet Isaiah, that our hearts might not settle for anything less than the coming of your reign. Give us the honesty of John the Baptist, that we might know our need for repentance and forgiveness. Give us the courageous joy of Mary, that we might become true disciples in spite of moments of uncertainty and sorrow. Lastly, dear God, give us patience, that we might wait in hope for all your gifts to us. AMEN.

Mark Neilsen

Advent (2)

Light of the World, enter the darkness of our hearts and renew us in faith, hope and love. As we prepare to celebrate the great mystery of the Incarnation, help us to see your presence in our world, especially in the needs of the poor. Strengthen us to become true peacemakers able to love our

enemies and forgive those who have offended us.
Lead us to acknowledge our own sinfulness, accept
your mercy and extend your healing love to those
around us. AMEN.

Advent (3)

Spirit of God, you stir our hearts in the Advent
season to awaken us from the spiritual doldrums.
You urge us to be alert to the coming of the Lord,
whether now or at the end of time. You invite us
to embrace our longing for the fullness of a life
without end. Enlighten our hearts with your holy
wisdom so that we might seek and find you, especially in the needs of the poor. Give us the courage
and perseverance to look for the Holy One, who
offers us more than the world can ever give. AMEN.

Advent (4)

Lord Jesus, you said that you came not to condemn
the world but that we might have abundant life.
Open my heart to receive the abundant life you
offer me this Advent season. Allow me to experience the wonder of a child looking forward to
Christmas for the first time. Strengthen my desire
for your coming that I might be renewed in heart,
mind and spirit as I prepare to celebrate your coming at Christmas. AMEN.

Christmas

Mighty and Eternal God, Power of the Universe,
you came among us as an infant to set us free from
fear. Sharing our life, you shared also our destiny,
accepting death on our behalf. As we celebrate the
wonderful mystery of God-With-Us, help us to see
the value of our lives from your point of view. May
we cherish all human life and support one another
as we journey together toward our final destiny in
you. Grant us a share of your love that we might
more fully love one another. AMEN.

Epiphany

Dear Jesus, a star in the heavens drew three men from the East to your manger so long ago; let my heart be drawn to you now. They knelt before you in homage; help me now to absorb some of the wonder of God become a tiny baby. The wise men brought gifts of gold, frankincense and myrrh; grant me the generosity to give back some of what you have given me in service to others. Most of all, may the example of these three ancient seekers encourage me never to become willing to settle for less than your true presence. AMEN.

Lent (1)

O God, help me begin this season of Lent with a right attitude. I trust that you will guide and support my Lenten observances. Help me practice works of charity and sacrifice in the spirit of gracious giving rather than self-punishment. May I remain solemn without becoming sullen, keeping in my heart the promise of Easter. AMEN.

Nancy F. Summers

Lent (2)

Lord, you endured forty days of temptation and suffering. Lead me into the desert as you did the children of Israel. Change my contrite heart, and help me grow in holiness. Guide my steps of sacrifice to Calvary and beyond the empty tomb. May I rise with you on Easter to a new life of grace. I ask this in your name. AMEN.

Lent (3)

May all I do this Lent
help me to truly repent,
to meditate and to pray
each and every day. AMEN.

Lent (4)

O Lord, Lent is a time to stop the mindless bustle and see where I stand with you. I need to know where I am lacking in my response to you. When I get that right, when I am closer to you, I know that my relationship with others can also deepen and flower. Help me to understand your ways of love and put them into practice. AMEN.

Jean Royer

Lent (5)

God our Father, grant that we who meditate on the Passion and death of your Son, Jesus Christ, may imitate in our lives his love and his self-giving by our love and service to you and to others. We ask this through Christ our Lord. AMEN.

Holy Week

Lord, as we contemplate your Passion, death and resurrection, help us to realize that you understand what suffering means to us. You were betrayed by one friend and abandoned by others. You felt the sting of the whip and the pain of mockery and humiliation. And you wondered where the Father was in the midst of your trial. As we remember how you endured all this out of love for us, may our hearts be moved to love you in return. AMEN.

Easter

Lord Jesus, when you rose on Easter morning, you brought new life to the world. May a share of that new life be ours today as we go forth to love and serve you in our brothers and sisters, especially the least among us. Fill us with every grace and blessing so that we might be your presence in the world. May your will be done in us. AMEN.

Pentecost

Holy Spirit, enlighten me with your truth, guide me with your understanding, strengthen me with your courage, console me with your love and keep me secure in hope. AMEN.

A Winter Prayer

Lord, you bring the cold winds with the gentle rains. Before the earth springs into new life, you give it a season of stillness and death. Silence the voices of busyness in our hearts, and open our ears to hear your voice. In Christ's name, AMEN.

For the Springtime

Creator God, thank you for the gift of nature and the world of plants and animals that emerge anew each spring. In the goodness of the natural world, we see your creative touch and your desire for abundant life. Help us to savor these days of growth and to look in our hearts for that same creative touch within. AMEN.

For Summer Mornings

O God, when birds wake the world with their songs of life and the sun warms the earth, it is easy to be aware of your presence. Before I get busy and it slips from my mind, help me to use these precious moments to be totally with you. May your name be praised today in my heart and all over the world. AMEN.

Steve Givens

An Autumn Prayer

Thank you, generous Creator, for the autumn leaves. What a wonderful gift to give us as we await the onset of winter! The dying trees and flowers remind us of our own mortality, and we feel the cold breath of time blowing past us. And you, knowing our weakness and fear, give us this glorious beauty—not just one magnificent tree, but a world full of glowing leaves! You remind us of your boundlessness, of your power to bring beauty out of every situation. Help me to commit my life and my hope to your loving care. AMEN.

Denise Barker

For the Coming Harvest

Lord, in the rhythm of the seasons, we find a revelation of your beauty and goodness. Grant us the mercy of cleansing rain, the fertility of rich soil and the bounty of steady growth. Strengthen the hands of the farmers and all those whose labor helps to bring food to our tables. Through your mercy, may we have enough nourishment to strengthen our bodies and enough love to share what we have with those in need. AMEN.

For a Season of Success

Lord, we have planted the seed, tended the shoots and watered the leaves. Now it is up to you to grant us the yield of our labors. May we accept all things from your hands in gratitude and confidence that you give us only what is best. Help us to share our abundance and to reach out to others. May those in need always have a place at our table. We ask all this in the name of Jesus. AMEN.

In Preparation for the Holidays

Lord, help me prepare for the holiday season this
year without turning it into a long laundry list
of obligations, deadlines and expectations. May
I never forget that all my plans are just so much
dust unless they are rooted in your will. Remind
me that you have already come, and that in the
fullness of time, your Kingdom will be revealed. As
these days of preparation and celebration unfold,
keep me alert to your presence. Make me aware
of the chances I have to bring your love to those
around me, especially those most in need. AMEN.

In Thanks *and* Praise

A Prayer of Thanksgiving

Lord, thank you for life:
> we live as your Church,
> in faith and hope.

Lord, thank you for love:
> we love in our families,
> in work and in play.

Lord, thank you for prayer:
> we pray in our joy and our sorrow,
> in laughter and silence.

Lord, thank you for this world:
> we delight in rainbows and skyscrapers,
> sand dunes and icicles,
> friendships and music.

Lord, thank you. AMEN.

Julia DiSalvo

In Thanksgiving for Faith

Lord, I praise you not only for the blessings of my life, but for the many ways that you have turned sorrow into joy and weakness into strength. You have promised to be with us always, and your constant presence benefits us in ways that become clear only with time. I pray especially in gratitude for the gift of faith, something I could never have constructed or maintained on my own. AMEN.

In Gratitude

Thank you, Lord, for the blessings of my life, especially the one I am calling to mind right now. Whenever I get discouraged, remind me of your goodness and fidelity in moments like this. When I am close to despair, turn my heart toward you and away from myself. AMEN.

In Praise (1)

Maker of heaven and earth, I give you praise for all
that sustains us in body and soul. For the nourishment of bread and the joy of wine, the satisfaction
of work and the exhilaration of music, I glorify
your name. Your creative hand is evident in all the
gifts you provide. You entice us into your presence
that we might have life to the full. Even in this
prayer of praise, you offer me the gift of wisdom in
knowing the source of all that is good. AMEN.

In Praise (2)

Praise to you, Lord Jesus, for you have set us free to
share your life for all eternity. AMEN.

For Life

O God, our Creator, all life is in your hands from conception until death. Help us to cherish our children and to reverence the awesome privilege of our share in creation. May all people live and die in dignity and love. Bless all those who defend the rights of the unborn, the handicapped and the aged. Enlighten and be merciful toward whose who fail to love, and give them peace. Let freedom be tempered by responsibility, integrity and morality. We ask all this in Jesus' name. AMEN.

For Stewardship

Good and generous God, help me to serve you today in what I do as well as in what I am. Show me the way to use the time, talent and treasure I have in order to be a light for the world, and so give glory to your name. Open my heart to the needs of those around me so that I take the time to listen and to respond with kindness rather than impatience. AMEN.

For the Gift of the Blessed Mother

Lord Jesus, you gave your mother Mary to the Church to encourage us to persevere in tough times. Instill in us now the desire to draw near to her and receive her motherly care. The first to bear you into the world, may she continue to inspire us to follow you in humility and openness to the workings of the Holy Spirit. May we always realize that our devotion to her will never lead us astray but always point us back to you. Help us take to heart her words to the wine stewards at the wedding feast at Cana: "Do whatever he tells you."

AMEN.

For the Pope

Good Shepherd, we pray for your protection and
guidance over our Holy Father. Give him strength
and wisdom to stand as a prophet for our times.
May he be a light in darkness around which we
gather in hope. We ask you to bring about reconciliation through his faithful teaching of peace and
justice. Grant him compassion and care to live the
gospel in love and service to all people. Let him
follow in the path of Peter and Paul who, filled
with the Holy Spirit, preached that the Lord saves
all who call upon his name. AMEN.

For the Church

Guide and protect your Church, O Lord, as you
have promised to do. May the Church be bold in
proclaiming the Good News of Christ, and may it
be firm in teaching all the sacred truths entrusted
to it. Above all, may we, the Church, strive always
to be humble and repentant, realizing that while
on our pilgrimage here "we see in a mirror, dimly"
(1 Corinthians 13:12) and will only know you fully

in eternity when we are united in heaven as the Church triumphant. AMEN.

For the Country

Almighty God, thank you for this country I call home. I often fail to see how blessed we are. Thank you for the opportunities that have allowed us to achieve so much for so many. Thank you for the yet-untapped material and spiritual resources that hold the rich potential for even greater achievements. May we accept these gifts in deep gratitude and use them for good. AMEN.

For Refugees and Victims of Natural Disaster

Almighty and eternal God, grant peace and material aid to the people of lands ravaged by war or natural disaster. May our hearts be moved to reach out to them in prayer and to offer whatever support we can. As they struggle for survival, may we gain courage and hope to become more effective partners for them tomorrow. AMEN.

For the Unemployed

Lord Jesus, you know what it means to make a living by the work of your hands. Your first disciples made a living from the sea and from commerce. Strengthen those who are unable to find gainful employment. Give them the encouragement they need to keep looking, the creativity to seek out new opportunities and the self-confidence to know they have something to offer. Bless the work of our hands, O Lord, and may we do your will in all things. AMEN.

For Mothers

Loving and merciful God, thank you for all the dear women who bring life into the world, especially the one who gave birth to me. With caring embraces, wisdom and guidance, a mother prepares her children to give their gifts to the world. Grant them patience and courage as they do the hard work of lovingly raising children. Give them hope amid all the world's turmoil and trust in your eternal care for each one of us. AMEN.

For Fathers

Father in heaven, you have promised to strengthen, guide and sustain us in your way. Grant all fathers the same determination to do the same for their children. Help them to love tenderly, discipline firmly and accept warmly the children with which you have blessed them. Give them the support of wife, family and friends as they offer their fidelity and love to their children and to the world.

AMEN.

For Children

Lord, bless all children with the loving care of conscientious parents. Protect them from all that would steal their childhood from them, and guide them to seek and find you, the source of all lasting joy. AMEN.

For Teenagers

O Lord, bless all the young who are growing up
in this world. They are the promise of the future
family, the future Church, the future world. Guide
their idealism and energy, their need to take their
lives into their own hands as adults, their openness to the rich variety of your creation. Give
them confidence, hope and gentle hearts. Protect
them from discouragement and cynicism, and from
counterfeit values. Give them, above all, the courage to take up their responsibilities, the wisdom to
absorb the best of the past and the happiness that
comes from faith in you. AMEN.

For Children Grown and Gone

Lord Jesus, I can still remember when they filled
the house. I remember when they were babies and
when they were teenagers. I remember when I
shouted at them and scolded, and when they were
angry with me. I remember, too, how my heart
ached with love for them, as it still does today.

Thank you for my children, now living lives of

their own. Be with them, Jesus, and give them your Holy Spirit in abundant measure, to guard and guide them. Send your angels to protect them, and may our Blessed Mother watch over them. Keep them close to you, O Lord, even if I may not understand your ways of doing that. Thank you again, Lord, for my children, grown and gone.

AMEN.

Mitch Finley

For Families

God, Our Father, loving and merciful, we pray for the needs of families: for abundant love, for forgiveness and reconciliation, for a living faith to face the challenges of each day. Jesus, you know what families need to nourish both children and parents in long-lasting bonds of loving service and mutual respect. Help families of all shapes and sizes turn to you as their source of life. Holy Spirit, encourage husbands and wives, mothers and fathers, brothers and sisters, and give them all the eyes to appreciate one another. Help us all to be grateful for the gift of families. AMEN.

For Veterans of the Armed Forces

Almighty and eternal God, bless those who have served their country in the military. May they know how much their service is appreciated by their fellow citizens. Grant those who are recently returned from active combat deep healing and a sense of peace as they resume their civilian lives. May our nation give them the honor and support they need throughout their lives. AMEN.

For Healing
and Help

For Healing

Gracious Lord, remember in your mercy those who suffer today. Give strength and encouragement to those who minister to their needs. Remember your promise not to let them be tested beyond what they are able to bear. Above all, give them the reassurance that you are with them as they walk through this valley of the shadows of death. And in your good time send healing of body and spirit. [Name those who need healing or help in their suffering.] In Jesus' name, AMEN.

For the Sick

God of mercy, when I'm sick I often find it hard to pray. So I offer this moment of prayer when I'm well for all those who may now be too weak, too tired or too depressed to pray and to believe at this time in your goodness and mercy. May this be a healing moment for them, as it was for the woman in the Gospel who touched the hem of your garment. AMEN.

Sr. Marguerite Zralek, OP

For a Loved One Who Has Died

Lord, I pray for the repose of the soul of [name], whose death has left a hole in my life. May she/he rest in peace through your great mercy. Grant consolation to her/his family members and friends, and may we all join in the resurrection of the dead through Christ our Lord. AMEN.

For Confidence in Prayer

O Jesus, your disciples often found you at prayer, and so they asked you to teach them how to do it. Help me to pray in confidence to the Father, just as you did. When I am facing my own agony of doubt and fear, pray with me so that I find courage and hope. When my life leads me to the cross, take my hand so that my heart stays strong. Most of all, strengthen my resolve to pray: Not my will, but yours be done. AMEN.

For Confidence in the Future

Lord, you have been with me from the very beginning, and you will be there at the very end. Looking back over my life, I can see that you were with me even when I was unaware of your presence, guiding me and drawing me closer to you. Give me courage and confidence in my future, believing that your hand is upon me every day, whether I am aware of it or not. AMEN.

For Courage

Lord Jesus, you were an innocent victim of violence, and your courage in the face of death opened the way to eternal life for us. Open our hearts now to the Holy Spirit's gift of courage that we may receive new life without fear. AMEN.

For a Special Intention

Lord, you know what is weighing on my heart right now. If you want me to carry it, I will to the best of my ability. If you want to lift it from me, I will let it go. AMEN.

For Humility

O God, you have made us out of earth, so let me be content with being human. Your breath has given us life, so let me gratefully receive the divine spark within my soul. Help me to accept the truth of who I really am, loved into being and sent to serve humbly in your name. AMEN.

For Healing of Resentments

Lord, you know both the wounds I carry and the grudges I nurse. Bring healing to my heart so I don't have to endlessly revisit old pains and resentments. Help me to forgive, for my own peace of mind if nothing else. Remind me that when you forgive me, the past is released once and for all. May I let go of all the burdens of the past so I can live in joy today. AMEN.

For Contrition

Forgiving Father, open my heart to your mercy so that I might desire to be healed of sin and so become better able to love you and those around me. Dissolve the hardness of my heart so that I might seek to forgive others as I have been forgiven. Take away the pride that can sometimes blind me to my responsibility in the conflicts and divisions that disrupt peace at home, in school or at work. Give me courage to face the truth and make the right choices. AMEN.

For Encouragement

Lord, my spirits are at a low ebb due to circumstances beyond my control. I don't want to complain and mope all the time, but I am sorely tempted to do just that. Help me to acknowledge not only the difficulties I face, but also the strengths I have, especially the strength to choose my own attitude. Give me the virtue of courage to take action where I can change things for the better. Give me also the grace of acceptance without bitterness where I am powerless to make a difference. AMEN.

Everyday
Prayers

Come, Holy Spirit

V. Come, Holy Spirit, fill the hearts of your faithful

R. and kindle in us the fire of your love.

V. Send forth your Spirit, and we shall be created,

R. and you shall renew the face of the earth.

Let us pray:

O God, who by the light of the Holy Spirit instructs the hearts of the faithful, grant that by the same Holy Spirit we may be truly wise and ever rejoice in His consolations. Through Christ our Lord, AMEN.

Guardian Angel Prayer

Angel of God, my guardian dear,

to whom God's love commits me here,

ever this day be at my side,

to light and guard, to rule and guide. AMEN.

Grace Before Meals

Bless us, O Lord, and these, thy gifts which we are about to receive from thy bounty, through Christ, our Lord, AMEN.

Grace After Meals

We give you thanks, Almighty God, for all your benefits, who lives and reigns forever and ever. May the souls of the faithful departed, through the mercy of God, rest in peace. AMEN.

Act of Faith

O my God, I firmly believe that you are one God in three divine persons, Father, Son and Holy Spirit. I believe that your divine Son became man and died for our sins, and that he will come to judge the living and the dead. I believe these and all the truths which the holy catholic Church teaches, because in revealing them you can neither deceive nor be deceived. AMEN.

Act of Hope

O my God, relying on your almighty power and infinite mercy and promises, I hope to obtain pardon of my sins, the help of your grace and life everlasting, through the merits of Jesus Christ, my Lord and Redeemer. AMEN.

Act of Love/Charity

O my God, I love you above all things with my whole heart and soul, because you are all-good and worthy of all love. I love my neighbor as myself for the love of you. I forgive all who have injured me and ask pardon of all whom I have injured. AMEN.

Act of Contrition

O my God, I am heartily sorry for having offended you, and I detest all my sins because of your just punishment, but most of all because I have offended you, my God, who are all good and deserving of all my love. I firmly resolve, with the help of your grace, to sin no more and to avoid the near occasions of sin. AMEN.

The Serenity Prayer

God, grant me the serenity
to accept the things I cannot change,
the courage to change the things I can,
and the wisdom to know the difference. AMEN.

theologian Dr. Reinhold Niebuhr

Prayers *in* Scripture

The Beatitudes

Blessed are the poor in spirit,
    for theirs is the kingdom of heaven.
Blessed are those who mourn,
    for they will be comforted.
Blessed are the meek,
    for they will inherit the earth.
Blessed are those who hunger and thirst for righ-
        teousness,
    for they will be filled.
Blessed are the merciful,
    for they will receive mercy.
Blessed are the pure in heart,
    for they will see God.
Blessed are the peacemakers,
    for they will be called children of God.
Blessed are those who are persecuted for righteous-
        ness' sake,
    for theirs is the kingdom of heaven.

Matthew 5:3-10

Psalm 23

A psalm of David.

The LORD is my shepherd, I shall not want.
    He makes me lie down in green pastures;
he leads me beside still waters;
    he restores my soul.
He leads me in right paths
    for his name's sake.
Even though I walk through the darkest valley,
    I fear no evil;
for you are with me;
    your rod and your staff—
    they comfort me.
You prepare a table before me
    in the presence of my enemies;
you anoint my head with oil;
    my cup overflows.
Surely goodness and mercy shall follow me
    all the days of my life,
and I shall dwell in the house of the LORD
    my whole life long.

Magnificat (Canticle of Mary)

My soul magnifies the Lord,
    and my spirit rejoices in God my Savior,
for he has looked with favor on the lowliness of his
        servant.
    Surely, from now on all generations will call
        me blessed;
for the Mighty One has done great things for me,
    and holy is his name.
His mercy is for those who fear him
    from generation to generation.
He has shown strength with his arm;
    he has scattered the proud in the thoughts of
        their hearts.
He has brought down the powerful from their
        thrones,
    and lifted up the lowly;
he has filled the hungry with good things,
    and sent the rich away empty.
He has helped his servant Israel,
    in remembrance of his mercy,
according to the promise he made to our ancestors,
    to Abraham and to his descendants forever.

Luke 1:46-55

Surrendering to God's Will

Father, into your hands I commend my spirit.
Luke 23:46; see also Psalm 31:5

A Prayer of St. Paul

I bow my knees before the Father, from whom every family in heaven and on earth takes its name. I pray that, according to the riches of his glory, he may grant that you may be strengthened in your inner being with power through his Spirit, and that Christ may dwell in your hearts through faith, as you are being rooted and grounded in love. I pray that you may have the power to comprehend, with all the saints, what is the breadth and length and height and depth, and to know the love of Christ that surpasses knowledge, so that you may be filled with all the fullness of God... to him be glory in the church and in Christ Jesus to all generations, forever and ever. AMEN.

Ephesians 3:14-19, 21

Saints *and* Prayers

St. Michael, the Archangel

St. Michael the Archangel, defend us in battle; be our safeguard against the wickedness and snares of the devil.

May God rebuke him, we humbly pray, and may you, prince of the heavenly hosts, by the power of God, cast into hell Satan and all the fallen angels who wander through the world seeking the ruin of souls. AMEN.

Prayer of St. Francis

Lord, make me an instrument of your peace.
Where there is hatred, let me sow love;
where there is injury, pardon;
where there is doubt, faith;
where there is despair, hope;
where there is darkness, light;
and where there is sadness, joy.

Divine Master, grant that I may not so much seek
      to be consoled as to console;
to be understood as to understand;
to be loved as to love.
For it is in giving that we receive;
it is in pardoning that we are pardoned;
and it is in dying that we are born to eternal life.
                                    Amen.

St. Patrick's Breastplate

Christ with me, Christ before me,
Christ behind me, Christ in me,
Christ beneath me, Christ above me,
Christ on my right, Christ on my left,
Christ when I lie down, Christ when I sit down,
Christ when I arise.

I arise today through a mighty strength,
the invocation of the Trinity,
Through belief in the threeness,
Through confession of the oneness,
Of the Creator of Creation. Amen.

St. Joseph Prayer

Saint Joseph, we seek to make a home in our hearts for Jesus, and so we pray for the same courage and trust in God you showed as you cared for Mary and Jesus. Patron and protector of the family, you faithfully fulfilled your duties in the family and in your labor. Recognizing you as a model of a loving father and a faithful husband, we ask your prayers for us that we might welcome Jesus into our lives and faithfully follow him until the end of our days. AMEN.

Mark Neilsen

Prayers *of the* Rosary

Our Father

Our Father, who art in heaven,
hallowed be thy name;
thy kingdom come, thy will be done
on earth as it is in heaven.
Give us this day our daily bread,
and forgive us our trespasses
as we forgive those who trespass against us;
and lead us not into temptation,
but deliver us from evil. AMEN.

Hail Mary

Hail Mary, full of grace! the Lord is with thee;
blessed art thou among women,
and blessed is the fruit of thy womb, Jesus.

Holy Mary, Mother of God,
pray for us sinners
now and at the hour of our death. AMEN.

Glory Be (Doxology)

Glory be to the Father,
and to the Son,
and to the Holy Spirit.
As it was in the beginning,
is now,
and ever shall be,
world without end. AMEN.

Fatima Prayer
Recited after every decade.

O my Jesus, forgive us our sins, save us from the
fires of hell, and lead all souls to heaven, especially
those in most need of your mercy.

Sign of the Cross

In the name of the Father,
and of the Son,
and of the Holy Spirit. AMEN.

Apostles' Creed

I believe in God,
the Father almighty,
Creator of heaven and earth,
and in Jesus Christ, his only Son, our Lord;
who was conceived by the Holy Spirit,
born of the Virgin Mary,
suffered under Pontius Pilate,
was crucified, died and was buried;
he descended into hell;
on the third day he rose again from the dead;
he ascended into heaven,
and is seated at the right hand
of God the Father almighty;
from there he will come to judge
the living and the dead.

I believe in the Holy Spirit,
the holy catholic Church,
the communion of saints,
the forgiveness of sins,
the resurrection of the body,
and life everlasting. AMEN.

Hail, Holy Queen
(Salve Regina)

Hail, Holy Queen, Mother of Mercy,
our life, our sweetness and our hope!
To you do we cry, poor banished children of Eve;
to you do we send up our sighs,
mourning and weeping in this valley of tears.
Turn then, most gracious advocate,
your eyes of mercy toward us;
and after this, our exile,
show unto us the blessed fruit of your womb, Jesus.
O clement, O loving, O sweet Virgin Mary!

V. Pray for us, O Holy Mother of God,
**R. that we may be made worthy of the promises
     of Christ.**

Mysteries of the Rosary

Joyful Mysteries

Monday and Saturday

The Annunciation
The Visitation
The Nativity
The Presentation
Finding Jesus in the Temple

Sorrowful Mysteries

Tuesday and Friday

The Agony in the Garden
The Scourging at the Pillar
The Crowning with Thorns
The Carrying of the Cross
The Crucifixion

Glorious Mysteries

Wednesday and Sunday

The Resurrection
The Ascension
The Descent of the Holy Spirit (Pentecost)
The Assumption of Mary
The Coronation of Mary

Luminous Mysteries

Thursday

The Baptism in the Jordan
The Wedding at Cana
The Proclamation of the Kingdom
The Transfiguration
The Institution of the Eucharist (Last Supper)

Divine Mercy Chaplet

1. Sign of the Cross
2. Our Father
3. Hail Mary
4. Apostles' Creed
5. On the Large Beads (once per decade)
Eternal Father, I offer you the Body and Blood,
Soul and Divinity of Your Dearly Beloved Son,
Our Lord, Jesus Christ, in atonement for our sins
and those of the whole world.

6. On the Small Beads (ten times per decade)
For the sake of His sorrowful Passion, have mercy
on us and on the whole world.

7. Conclusion (three times)
Holy God, Holy Mighty One, Holy Immortal One,
have mercy on us and on the whole world.

Marian
Prayers

The Angelus

V. The Angel of the Lord declared unto Mary,
R. And she conceived of the Holy Spirit.
Hail Mary, etc…

V. Behold the handmaid of the Lord:
R. Be it done unto me according to your word.
Hail Mary, etc…

V. And the Word was made flesh,
R. And dwelt among us.
Hail Mary, etc…

V. Pray for us, O Holy Mother of God,
R. That we may be made worthy of the promises of Christ.

Let us pray:
Pour forth, we beseech you, O Lord, your grace into our hearts; that we, to whom the incarnation of Christ, your Son, was made known by the message of an angel, may by his Passion and Cross be brought to the glory of his Resurrection, through the same Christ, our Lord. AMEN.

Regina Coeli
(Queen of Heaven)

This replaces the Angelus during the Easter season.

Queen of Heaven, rejoice! *Alleluia!*
For he whom you were privileged to bear, *Alleluia!*
Has risen as he said. *Alleluia!*
Pray for us to God. *Alleluia!*

Rejoice and be glad, O Virgin Mary, *Alleluia!*
For the Lord has truly risen, *Alleluia!*

Let us pray:
O God, who by the resurrection of your Son, our
Lord Jesus Christ, has been pleased to give joy
to the whole world, grant, we beseech you, that
through the intercession of the Blessed Virgin
Mary, his mother, we may attain the joys of eternal
life. Through the same Christ, our Lord, AMEN.

Memorare

Remember, O most gracious Virgin Mary, that never was it known that anyone who fled to thy protection, implored thy help, or sought thy intercession was left unaided.

Inspired by this confidence, I fly unto thee, O Virgin of Virgins, my Mother. To thee I come, before thee I stand, sinful and sorrowful. O Mother of the Word Incarnate, despise not my petition, but in thy mercy hear and answer me. AMEN.

Miraculous Medal Inscription

As revealed by Our Lady to St. Catherine Labouré

O Mary, conceived without sin,
pray for us who have recourse to thee.

Prayers
to Jesus

The Stations of the Cross

Where physical stations are not available, one can pray before a crucifix and imagine following Jesus from station to station.

The brief meditations following these stations are offered as a guide to your own meditation or quiet prayer in the presence of the Passion and death of our Lord.

1. Jesus Is Condemned to Death

We adore you, O Christ, and we praise you,
because by your Holy Cross you have redeemed the world.

Jesus was sentenced to death even though he was guilty of no transgression. The jealousy of the Jewish leaders and the cowardice of the Roman authorities made him a victim. For our sake, he accepted their power over him.

Father, not my will but yours be done.

2. Jesus Takes Up His Cross

We adore you, O Christ, and we praise you,
**because by your Holy Cross you have redeemed
the world.**

*Though exhausted from his beating at the hands of the
Roman soldiers, Jesus was forced to carry the cross, the
instrument of his own execution. He carried it as well as
he could, giving an example to all who would follow him.*

Father, not my will but yours be done.

3. Jesus Falls the First Time

We adore you, O Christ, and we praise you,
**because by your Holy Cross you have redeemed
the world.**

*The weight of the cross and the difficulty of the jour-
ney became too much for Jesus, and he fell. His will-
ingness to accept an unjust death did not mean that it
would be easy or over quickly. He pulled himself up
and continued on.*

Father, not my will but yours be done.

4. Jesus Meets His Mother

We adore you, O Christ, and we praise you,
**because by your Holy Cross you have redeemed
the world.**

*Jesus could no more protect Mary from the pain she
suffered upon seeing him in torment than she could
save him now. In a way, they bore one another's suffering, as all parents and children sometimes do.*

Father, not my will but yours be done.

5. Simon of Cyrene Helps Jesus

We adore you, O Christ, and we praise you,
**because by your Holy Cross you have redeemed
the world.**

*Worried that Jesus might not survive the arduous trip
up to Calvary, the soldiers pressed Simon into helping
him. It is very likely that Simon didn't recognize the
great opportunity he had been given to cooperate in
Jesus' saving mission.*

Father, not my will but yours be done.

6. Veronica Wipes Jesus' Face

We adore you, O Christ, and we praise you,
**because by your Holy Cross you have redeemed
the world.**

*A woman traditionally called Veronica (meaning
"true image") offered a simple gesture of kindness
to the suffering Jesus. Her compassion serves as a
reminder that no act that relieves pain is too small or
insignificant.*

Father, not my will but yours be done.

7. Jesus Falls a Second Time

We adore you, O Christ, and we praise you,
**because by your Holy Cross you have redeemed
the world.**

*A second time Jesus is overwhelmed by the journey.
Again he manages to get up. How difficult it must
have been to summon the strength and courage to go
on, knowing full well what lay ahead!*

Father, not my will but yours be done.

8. Jesus Meets the Mourning Women

We adore you, O Christ, and we praise you, **because by your Holy Cross you have redeemed the world.**

Jesus tells the women to weep not for him, but for themselves and their children. He knew they mourned only for "show" and that their sorrow was hollow. Had their hearts been genuine, they would have mourned their own sinfulness.

Father, not my will but yours be done.

9. Jesus Falls a Third Time

We adore you, O Christ, and we praise you, **because by your Holy Cross you have redeemed the world.**

Falling for the third time under the crushing burden of the cross, Jesus must have been sorely tempted to just lie there. But he drew upon his remaining strength to persevere on his sacrificial journey.

Father, not my will but yours be done.

10. Jesus Is Stripped of His Clothing

We adore you, O Christ, and we praise you,
because by your Holy Cross you have redeemed the world.

Jesus felt the sharp agony of old wounds ripped open, adding to the indignity of being publicly stripped of his clothing. Totally vulnerable, totally bereft, he humbled himself on every level for our sake.

Father, not my will but yours be done.

11. Jesus Is Nailed to the Cross

We adore you, O Christ, and we praise you,
because by your Holy Cross you have redeemed the world.

Large nails driven through his hands and feet, Jesus suffered even more. The soldiers could have tied him to the cross and he would have died, but they chose this more cruel, more painful way. Still, he forgave them.

Father, not my will but yours be done.

12. Jesus Dies on the Cross

We adore you, O Christ, and we praise you,
**because by your Holy Cross you have redeemed
the world.**

*The age-old question asked of any suffering echoes
through the mystery of the Redemption: why? God,
become fully human in Jesus, accepts death in all its
suffering. Why does God will this and why is Jesus
obedient to the Father's will? The answer is found in
the mystery of God's love for each one of us.*

Father, not my will but yours be done.

13. Jesus Is Taken Down from the Cross

We adore you, O Christ, and we praise you,
because by your Holy Cross you have redeemed the world.

All life has flowed out, and now all that remains is Jesus' battered and abused body. A soldier pierces his side with a lance, just to make sure he is dead. They can hurt him no more.

Father, not my will but yours be done.

14. Jesus Is Laid in the Tomb

We adore you, O Christ, and we praise you,
because by your Holy Cross you have redeemed the world.

For his disciples, Jesus' death and burial meant the end of everything they had hoped for and all of their dreams. What remained were fragments of their faith. Their darkness would soon be transformed, not by their power, but by the glory of God.

Father, not my will but yours be done.

103

Prayer Before a Crucifix

Good and gentle Jesus, I kneel before you. I see and I ponder your five wounds. My eyes behold what David prophesied about you: "They have pierced my hands and feet; they have counted all my bones." Engrave on me this image of yourself. Fulfill the yearnings of my heart; give me faith, hope, and love, repentance for my sins, and true conversion of life. AMEN.

To the Sacred Heart of Jesus

I fly to you, Sacred Heart of my Savior, for you are my refuge, my only hope. You are the remedy for all my miseries, my consolation in all my wretchedness, the reparation for all my infidelities, the supplement for all my deficiencies, the expiation for all my sins, the hope and the end of all my prayers. You are the only one who is never weary of me and who can bear with my faults, because you love me with an infinite love. Therefore, O my God, have mercy on me according to your great mercy, and do with me, and for me and in me whatever you will, for I give myself entirely to you, Divine Heart, with full confidence that you will never reject me. AMEN.

Divine Praises

Recited or sung during Reposition of the Blessed Sacrament.

Blessed be God.
Blessed be His holy name.
Blessed be Jesus Christ, true God and true man.
Blessed be the name of Jesus.
Blessed be His Most Sacred Heart.
Blessed be His Most Precious Blood.
Blessed be Jesus in the Most Holy Sacrament of
      the Altar.
Blessed be the Holy Spirit, the Paraclete.
Blessed be the great Mother of God, Mary Most
      Holy.
Blessed be her Holy and Immaculate Conception.
Blessed be her glorious Assumption.
Blessed be the name of Mary, Virgin and Mother.
Blessed be St. Joseph, her most chaste spouse.
Blessed be God in His angels and in His saints.

AMEN.

Pange Lingua

*For the Solemnity of Corpus Christi or Holy Thursday. The
"Tantum Ergo" stanzas are used at Benediction.*

Sing, my tongue, the Savior's glory,
Of his Flesh the mystery sing;
Of the Blood, all price exceeding,
Shed by our immortal King,
Destined, for the world's redemption,
From a noble womb to spring.

Of a pure and spotless Virgin
Born for us on earth below;
He, as man, with man conversing,
Stayed, the seeds of truth to sow;
Then he closed in solemn order
Wondrously his life of woe.

On the night of that Last Supper,
Seated with his chosen band,
He, the Paschal victim eating,
First fulfills the Law's command;
Then as food to his Apostles
Gives himself with his own hand.

Word-made-Flesh, the bread of nature
By his word to Flesh he turns;
Wine into his Blood he changes,
What though sense no change discerns?
Only be the heart in earnest,
Faith her lesson quickly learns.

Tantum Ergo
Down in adoration falling,
Lo! the Sacred Host we hail;
Lo! o'er ancient forms departing:
Newer rites of grace prevail;
Faith for all defects supplying
Where the feeble senses fail.

To the everlasting Father,
And the Son who reigns on high,
With the Holy Ghost proceeding
Forth from each eternally,
Be salvation, honor, blessing,
Might, and endless majesty. AMEN.
    St. Thomas Aquinas, tr. by Edward Caswall (1814-1878)

Anima Christi

Soul of Christ, sanctify me.
Body of Christ, save me.
Blood of Christ, inebriate me.
Water from the side of Christ, wash me.
Passion of Christ, strengthen me.

O good Jesus, hear me.
Within Thy wounds, hide me.
Suffer me not to be separated from Thee.
From the malicious enemy, defend me.
In the hour of my death, call me,
And bid me come unto Thee,
That with Thy saints I may praise Thee forever
and ever, Amen.

Jesus Prayer

Lord Jesus Christ, Son of God,
have mercy on me, a sinner. Amen.

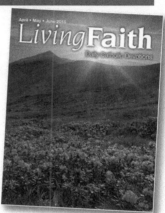